A *Day in the Life of a*
Victorian Child

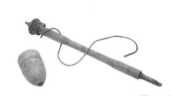

Contents

Time to get up 2

Breakfast 4

Walking to school 6

Working at school 8

Playing at school 10

Going home 12

Time for bed 14

Index 16

Time to get up

Edward jumps out of bed. He pours water from the jug into the wash bowl and washes himself. Then he puts on his clothes.

jug

wash bowl

Breakfast

The fire in the cooking range heats the kitchen. The porridge is cooked in a saucepan on top of the range.

saucepan

cooking range

Walking to school

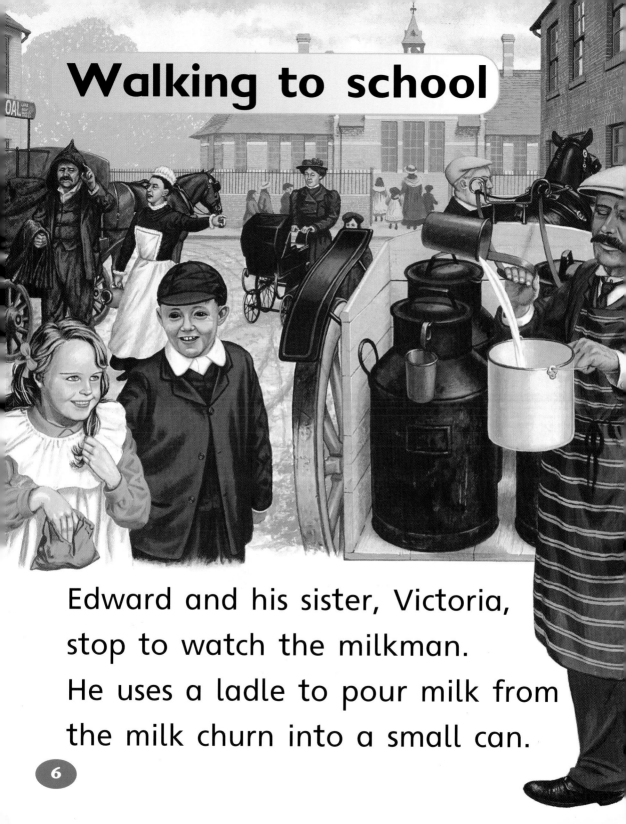

Edward and his sister, Victoria,
stop to watch the milkman.
He uses a ladle to pour milk from
the milk churn into a small can.

milk churn

ladle

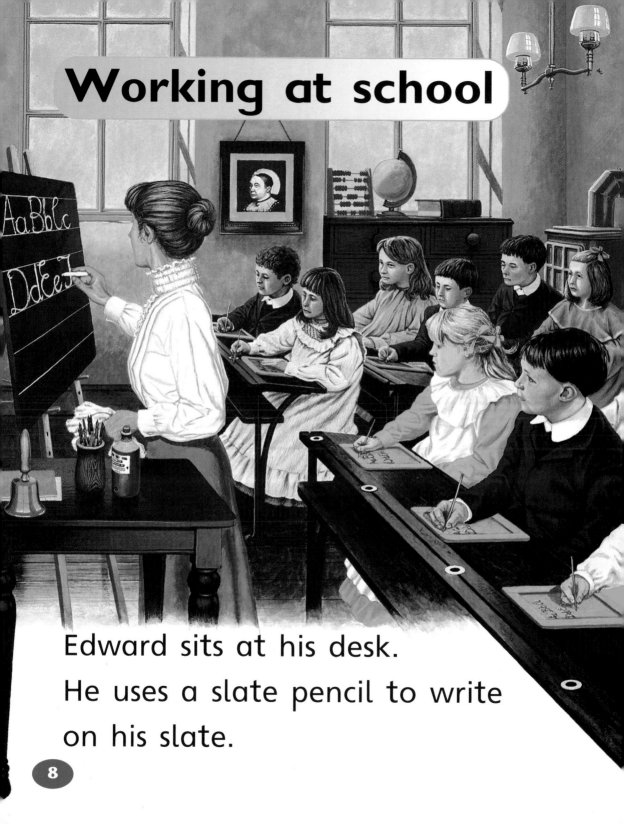

Working at school

Edward sits at his desk.
He uses a slate pencil to write
on his slate.

slate

slate pencil

Playing at school

Edward plays with his spinning top.
Victoria runs to catch her hoop.
Some children play hopscotch.

spinning top

hoop

Going home

After school Edward buys
some sweets. The shopkeeper
weighs the bag of sweets on the
scales. Edward gives him a penny.

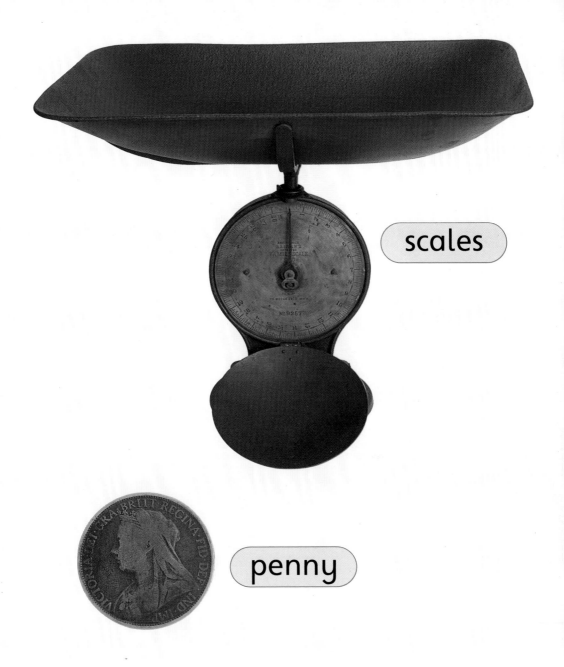

scales

penny

Time for bed

It is time for Edward to go to bed.
His mother takes a candle upstairs.
Edward takes his hot water bottle
to keep him warm.

hot water bottle

candle

Index

candle 14, 15

cooking range 4, 5

hoop 10, 11

hot water bottle 14, 15

jug 2, 3

ladle 6, 7

milk churn 6, 7

penny 12, 13

saucepan 4, 5

scales 12, 13

slate 8, 9

slate pencil 8, 9

spinning top 10, 11

wash bowl 2, 3